Dear Glynis,

I loved your book so much! I can honestly say [illegible] learned things that I have never known about cancer. You know, with all the medication needed and how tired you are when you have cancer. I like the cover of the book, also. It stands out and captures my eye. It really wanted me to read it! I also found that *Mrs. B Has Cancer* was really emotional at points and inspiring. I just might have to read it again. I was so into it that I finished it in just two days.

If possible, could you send me some more of your books? I really like them and that would be great.

Nicole A Beswetherick, 12 years old

Mrs. B Has Cancer explores the emotional journey of Tristan's teacher going through cancer and everything else that goes along with it. I could feel Tristan's pain as he tried to help her the best he could.

From this book, you also learn a lot about what a chemo patient endures daily while going through treatment.

I would highly recommend *Mrs. B Has Cancer* to both children and adults.

Trenton Newton, 12 years old

Mrs. B Has Cancer

Mrs. B Has Cancer

Glynis M. Belec

Angel Hope Publishing

Mrs. B Has Cancer

Second Edition 2018

This book is a work of fiction, although it is based on a true story. The letter [pg.27] to Mrs. B is an actual letter written by a student.

ISBN: 978-0-9920074-0-9
Printed in Canada

Angel Hope Publishing
www.glynismbelec.com

Innovative Print
innovativeprint.ca

Cover Design by Thirteen 13 Designz
Amanda Belec
www.instagram.com/thirteen13designz

For Kyle, Brandon and Amanda and all my other precious students who asked questions and wondered.

Table of Contents

Chapter 1 THE NEWS

School stinks. My name is Tristan and they call me an ADHD kid. Mrs B, my tutor, tells me that ADHD stands for Absolutely Dependable Happy Dreamer. I like that.

I know one thing. Sitting still in my seat all day in school is really hard. There`s too much noise and buzzing from the lights and computers and stuff. And when someone talks to me, I`ve gotta' answer. Mr. Sparks, my teacher, doesn`t agree.

I'm not dumb but sometimes I have trouble learning some of the stuff in class. That's why I have to go to Mrs. B's.

Mrs. B called last night and Mom talked to her for ages. Today, when I went for my tutoring time, I could tell something was wrong. Mrs. B was smiling, but it was a sad smile, if that's even possible.

Mom came in with me today. I thought something was weird when she didn't just drop me off at the door like she usually does. There was a bit of a creepy silence. At first I thought I was in trouble, not sure what for— but both Mom and Mrs. B had that look on their faces. Then Mrs. B spoke.

"I have cancer," she said, "and I won't be able to teach you for a while."

"Cancer?" I looked at Mom.

I was sort of speechless for a second. I don't know much about cancer. But I do know that my grandpa had cancer and he died. Graham Deeble's mom had cancer and she died, too. They lived down the road from us. Then after his mom died, he and his dad moved away. I missed hanging out with Graham. Mrs. B used to tutor Graham for a while. I remember how sad she was when she found out about his mom.

My stomach gurgled. Then my tutoring life flashed before me like a YouTube video. I thought about that day when I couldn't sit still to do my spelling.

Mrs. B said, "Tristan, stand on your head and spell 'basket'."

"B-A-S-K-E-T."

"Right!"

"Ask me another word," I said.

"Picnic."

"P-I-C-N-I-C."

"Right again!"

When I couldn't understand how to do fractions, Mrs. B pulled out a chocolate bar from her secret drawer and told me to break it into two pieces.

"How many halves are in one whole chocolate bar?"

"Two."

"Right!"

"Now break the chocolate bar into 12 pieces. How many twelfths are in a whole?"

'Twelve."

"Right again! If you eat eight-twelfths of the chocolate bar, how much is left?"

"Four-twelfths," I mumbled with a mouthful of chocolate.

"That's the right answer!"

I really like doing fractions with Mrs. B.

For some dumb reason I started thinking about the day she told me how her niece gave her an aquarium. Six crazy fish swam in the bluish-green water. They were fun to watch, but the water smelled a little like my stinky hockey bag after a game.

"Let's have a 'name- the- fish' contest," Mrs. B had said

She had made up a special contest worksheet with a photograph of each fish and a line beside each one, so me and all her other students could write down our ideas.

"When we've named all the fish, we'll write a story about them," she had said.

I had decided to write a funny fish story. I remember thinking Mrs. B would like it because she likes to laugh.

"It's okay. Don't worry," Mrs. B said.

I think she could tell I was about to cry. Mom looked sad too, which didn't help.

"But I don't want you to die. Are you gonna die?" I asked.

"People don't always die from cancer," Mrs. B said.

I'd forgotten about spelling or fractions. I hadn't even looked at the fish.

"What's cancer?" I asked.

Mom wasn't saying much. She looked at Mrs. B.

"Do you remember when we talked last week about the body?"

I thought about the science lesson. I thought about how she said we were made in such a cool way.

"Remember the homework I gave you about cells? Those pictures you had to label and color?'

"Yes," I said, trying to remember that song Mrs. B made up about the body:

Cells make up the body. Yes, they do
Cells join together to make some tissue too.
Tissue works together and organs soon appear
Stomach, liver, pancreas and other structures near!

"Right!" said Mrs. B, after joining in with me. "You have a good memory. And the different organs have different jobs. The heart pumps our blood; the stomach and intestines help us digest food; our lungs help us breathe; and our immune system helps fight disease."

Blah, blah, blah. I really didn't want to review all that stuff, but I did remember the stomach we made out of bubblegum. That was fun, especially when it blew up because Jamie poked it with a pen.

Everything went too quiet again. So I asked a question. Mrs. B is always telling me to ask questions, so I did.

"What does all that stuff have to do with cancer? Why do we have to talk about science right now?"

Mrs. B sat on the stool next to me.

"Sometimes bad things happen to cells in a person's body. These bad cells harm an organ and then the person gets cancer. That's what happened to me."

"Are your organs sick now?"

"Yes. I have two big lumps called tumors on my ovaries. This is where the bad cells are."

"But why did the bad cells grow?"

"I`m not sure why it happened, but I do know one thing." Mrs. B was smiling at me and she gently touched my shoulder. "I'm feeling lots of love and lots of people are praying for me."

“Do you have to go to the hospital? I don’t like hospitals. I went to see Grandpa in the hospital when he was sick.”

“Yes. I have to go to the hospital. I have already had some tests, but I need to have more and then I’ll have an operation, which is called surgery.

“Can’t you have a needle or some medicine to make you better? When I had a cold, I had to take this purple stuff.”

“There is a medicine called chemotherapy that the doctor can give me to help fight the cancer, but he told me I probably would not need it. He said he thinks they can take away all the cancer when I am having the surgery. But we`ll have to wait and see.”

I was happy to hear that. Mrs. B told me she’d be sore after the surgery for a while, but the nurses would give her a different kind of medicine to take away the pain.

Mom and Mrs. B talked about stuff for a while. I wanted to leave and run away and not think about cancer. I walked over to the aquarium and watched the cool, colored fish flip and swim. Some were hiding in the green ferns. A blue one stuck its head out of the plastic shipwreck sitting on the bottom. A big brown thing was sucking the glass on the side. Its mouth made a perfect O shape.

“Are you okay?” Mom said a little while later. I looked at her. She came over to me and touched my shoulder.

I wanted to ask a million questions. I wanted to help make the cancer go away.

Chapter 2 TESTING ONE, TWO, THREE

"What kind of tests did you have?" I asked.

Mrs. B wiggled her finger and patted the stool next to her. I sat down. Mom went back to the 'waiting couch.'

"I had something called an ultrasound first. Do you know what that is?"

I thought about Gillian, my baby sister. I remembered the blackish pictures that were on the front of the fridge for a long time.

"I think so."

I looked at Mom.

"Isn't that what you had when Gillian was inside you?"

"Yes," she said. "You're right. Very good that you remembered, Tristan."

Mom had stuck on a little paper arrow that pointed to Gillian's head in the picture, because I couldn't see anything. I looked at Mom. I looked at Mrs. B.

"Are you gonna have a baby?"

Mrs. B and Mom both laughed.

"I'm a little too old to have babies. Besides, why do I need any more children? I have all of you to keep me busy."

Mrs. B waved her hand at the photos of her students on the wall.

"The test I had is called an ultrasound. But Mom had an ultrasound to check how Gillian was doing before she was born. I had the same test, but for a different reason."

I guess I was glad that Mrs. B was not having a baby. She was a little old for that. That would be too weird.

"Does an ultrasound hurt?" I asked.

"Not one little bit. In fact, it tickles," said Mrs. B. "All I had to do was lie down on a bed in a dark room, and then the person who was doing the test took out a little hard plastic wand. It was attached to a computer screen. She put some warm jelly on the wand and then rubbed it over my stomach area. Pictures popped on the screen. It took about twenty minutes and then I could go home."

"What did they see?"

"I guess they saw some shadows that they thought might be a tumor or cancer. That's when the doctor decided I should go for more tests."

"What other tests?"

"A CAT scan. Do you know what that is?

I hadn't a clue.

"Nope," I said as I watched Mrs. B draw something on a piece of paper. "What's that?"

Mrs. B pointed to the picture. "This is what a CAT scan machine looks like."

"What does it do?"

I'm surprised Mrs. B didn't tell me to look up CAT scan on the Internet or in an encyclopedia. She usually tells me to look up things I don't understand. But today she wanted me close to her. It made me feel better.

"This kind of test is not one that I had to study for, but I did have to get my body ready for it.

"How come it's called a CAT scan?" I wondered.

"First of all it has nothing to do with cats. The name CAT scan is short for Computerized Axial Tomography."

Those are big words. I tried to say them. "Computerized and Axion tomgra..."

Mrs. B laughed. "Almost right. Just say CAT scan. It's easier! It's a special sort of x-ray that can look for things in your body."

"What sort of things?"

"A CAT scan can tell the doctors and nurses if there are bad cells growing."

"What happened? Did it hurt?"

"First I had to drink a big drink that tasted like a really thin orange milkshake, without the ice-cream."

A milkshake wouldn't hurt very much.

"Then the people who work in the CAT scan department had me lie down on a skinny bed. Then they poked me in the arm with a needle so that they could put a special color or dye in my arm. That's called an intravenous or an IV."

Mrs. B drew a needle and an arm on the paper and showed me where they had poked her.

"Ouch! That must have been the part that hurt."

"A little, but I thought about good things as they poked me and I tried to relax. Then it wasn't so bad."

I don't know if I could be that brave if I ever had to have a needle poked into my arm. Mrs. B explained that once the needle was in, it didn't hurt anymore. They taped it in place so that it wouldn't slip out.

"The bed started to move slowly forward, and I went inside this hole." Mrs. B pointed to the picture again.

"It looks like a giant donut," I said.

Mrs. B and Mom laughed again. Mom got up off the waiting couch and came over to look at the picture.

"The machine talked to me and told me to hold my breath, and then it told me when to breathe again. It also had funny smiley faces on top of the machine that showed me what to do."

I like smiley faces. Mrs. B draws them all the time on my homework book. So if I went inside the giant donut, then maybe I would think of Mrs. B and homework. Okay maybe not homework.

"Did you have to lie still?" I said.

"Yes, I had to keep very still so the technicians could take pictures from the computer room behind me. I thought about all the good things I have in my life. That helped me to keep still. And then I pretended I was in a rocket ship."

I laughed when she said that. She knows that I like rocket ships and that one day I'm going to be an astronaut. Mrs. B said I have to work really hard to do that. I will.

"Will you have other tests?"

"Yes. I need to have lots of blood work done. That's when I get poked in the vein again and then they take out some blood and check it."

"Yuck. That doesn't sound like fun."

"Do you need a bone scan too?" Mom asked.

"What's a bone scan?" I wanted to know.

"Yes, I do," said Mrs. B to Mom. Mrs. B looked at me again.

"A bone scan is done with a big machine that has a camera. It kind of looks like a donut hole too. Like the CAT scan, they'll put a special dye in my arm. The only difference is when they inject the dye, I have to wait for three hours before the test."

"Does it take the same kind of pictures as the CAT scan?"

"No. Now the machine will look at my bones instead of my organs. A big camera goes over and under my body. While it's happening, I can't wriggle at all. If I do, they might see two heads!"

I laughed but I felt sorry for Mrs. B.

"I'll have my surgery next week, but I wanted you to come today with Mom so I could tell you why we'll have a break from tutoring."

Mom smiled and reached out for Mrs. B's hand.

Mrs. B had tears in her eyes. I'll really miss her, but I won't mind not having to do any homework for a while. Maybe I'll finish naming the fish on the page she gave me. That'll make her happy. I might even write a story about the fish. She'll be surprised if I do that.

It was hard to say goodbye to Mrs. B today. She asked me to pray for her, and I will. She said she would pray for me to be strong, and I know she will. She gave Mom and me a big hug. Mom is gonna' miss her too, I can tell. I hope we can visit Mrs. B when she's in the hospital.

Chapter 3 OPERATION HOSPITAL

Mrs. B had her surgery. Mom asked if I wanted to come when she visited her. I was a little afraid, but I wanted to see Mrs. B too.

When we arrived at the hospital my hands were shaking. I looked at Mom. She smiled at me and told me everything would be okay. The last time I came to a hospital, I saw Grandpa when he had cancer. He looked old and sick. I never saw him again until the funeral.

Seeing Mrs. B in hospital would be scary, but I wanted to show her that I was brave.

"You don't have to go, Tristan. We can turn around and go home. Maybe you can mail the card instead," said Mom.

I remember when Mrs. B told me that I needed to be brave to be an astronaut. I would be brave for Mrs. B.

"No, I want to see her," I said. I clutched my homemade card and walked next to Mom.

We took the elevator up to the fourth floor and went to the nursing station where Mom asked for Mrs. B's room number. A sharp cleaner-like smell made my nose twitch as we headed for room 409.

Mrs. B looked different. She was hooked up to a machine and had a plastic tube in her nose. I felt like crying when I saw her. But when she smiled I felt better. She tugged at her crinkly white sheets and sat up in her bed.

"Tristan, you came. She moved up in bed a little and tried to smooth out the crinkles. It's so good to see you. How are you?"

Mrs. B said hello to my mom and then reached out to touch my hand. I pulled away at first.

"Don't worry, Tristan. You can't catch cancer. It's not that kind of disease."

Sheesh...how did she know I was thinking that?

She stuck out her hand again. This time I held her hand for a few seconds. It felt warm and soft.

"Thanks for coming. Now I feel a lot better."

I was glad I helped Mrs. B feel better by coming up to see her in the hospital.

"Here, this is for you," I said, putting the card on the bed in front of her. Mrs. B's face lit up like candles on a birthday cake. She read it aloud.

Dear Mrs. B. I hope you have a good surgery, but you might be in pain. The pain will stop eventually. So I am wishing that you will be okay. You're in my heart all the time. When you come back, you might be in a little bit of pain, but trust me, it will stop eventually. So I hope that the big lumps are gone. Tristan

Mrs. B had tears in her eyes. I looked at my Mom. She had tears in her eyes too. I felt like crying a little bit, but someone had to stay strong.

"Thank you so much for this lovely card," said Mrs. B. Her voice wasn't very loud. "You have given me a good reason to hurry up and get better."

She took my hand again and squeezed it. She didn't say anything else but I knew she was happy. I'm glad I cheered her up.

"What's that machine for?" I asked. It was a cream-colored box attached to the long silver pole. It had lots of lights and buttons and made hissing sounds.

"It's called a pain pump. It's attached to the IV, and when I have pain, I just press a little button and the medicine comes out and flows into my vein. Then I'm not sore anymore."

"Is that when the needle goes into your vein like you were telling me about before?"

"Uh, huh." Mrs. B looked kind of weak.

"And what's that tube thing in your nose? Does it hurt?"

"No." Mrs. B took a deep breath and smiled. "It doesn't hurt at all. It's oxygen. It helps me breathe easier. After my surgery, the nurses make sure I have enough oxygen in my blood by giving me this. They put a little clip on my finger and it tells them when I have enough oxygen. It doesn't hurt at all when they put the clip on. When my oxygen level gets high enough, then I won't need this tube in my nose anymore."

"Cool." All this equipment was interesting.

"Look at all you're learning. Shall I give you some homework?"

Mom laughed. Mrs. B had a smile on her face. I wasn't sure if she was serious.

"Um, not really," I didn't want to hurt Mrs. B's feelings, but I didn't want any homework either.

"I'm just kidding," Mrs. B said.

I noticed that she pressed the button on her pain pump a few times. But she was still smiling at me. I think Mom noticed her do it too.

‘We should go now. Mrs. B needs to rest,” Mom said.

“Thanks again for the card, Tristan. I’ll keep it in a special place.”

We said goodbye to Mrs. B. I knew it would be a while before I would see her again. She told us she had to wait for two weeks, then she had to visit the doctor again. He would tell her how the surgery went and if she needed to have that special medicine she called chemotherapy. She said she did not think she would have to have it because they said her surgery went well. The doctor took away the lumps.

I was glad we went to visit Mrs. B. When you help someone to feel better, it’s neat how you begin to feel better too. When I left the hospital my hands weren’t shaking anymore.

Chapter 4 SLEEPOVER

"Tristan. Can you come into the living room?"

I heard Mom calling but I was pretty heavy into texting my friend, Jamie Jackson.

"Just a minute," I said. I had one more thing to tell him.

I looked at Jamie's last text.

LOL

We had been planning a sleepover after our ball game tomorrow night. He just finished telling me that we were going to beat the daylights out of the Blues. We were laughing, because so far this year, we are the worst team. We've only won one game out of six. I typed LOL back, then I told him I had to go.

I'll let you know for sure about you sleeping over ☺ I wrote. I was thinking that Mom would probably let me have Jamie over.

"Tristan. Are you coming?"

I walked into the living room and flopped into the recliner.

"I'm here." I grinned at Mom. She smiled back.

"I just got off the phone with Mrs. B."

Every night I think of Mrs. B. That's probably dumb, but I even think about her when I am in school and having some troubles with math or those dumb adjective and adverb things, or whatever they're called. It was a pain getting extra homework from Mrs. B, but I guess she did help me figure stuff out. I hate that she has cancer.

"What'd she say?" I asked.

"Remember how Mrs. B told us that her surgery went well and she didn't think she would need that special medicine?"

I thought about what that medicine was called.

"Um…you mean cheming...apy or something like that?"

"Chemotherapy," Mom said.

I nodded.

"Mrs. B went to the cancer doctor yesterday. She stopped speaking for a moment and

looked at me. "It turns out that she does have to have chemotherapy."

"You mean they didn't take away all the cancer?"

"Yes, that's right." Mom said. She didn't smile. She stared at me for a second.

What was I supposed to say? I didn't even know how I felt.

"Does that mean Jamie can't stay overnight tomorrow?"

As soon as I said it, I knew it was a dumb thing to say.

"What?" Mom smiled.

"Of course he can stay over, if it's okay with his parents," Mom said.

"What about Mrs. B?" I said.

"You want her to stay overnight too?" Mom and I laughed.

"No. That's not what I mean. I don't know what I mean."

Mom told me not to worry, and she told me a little bit about the treatment Mrs. B needed.

"Is that chemotherapy stuff a pill or like cough medicine?"

"It's a special medicine that helps fight the cancer, but instead of swallowing it, it's given in the vein through an IV — like Mrs. B had in her arm after surgery. Remember?"

I remembered. Mom looked serious so I was quiet and listened.

"The medicine might make her feel a little sick at first, and she'll probably feel very tired
for a while."

"If it's medicine, why will it make her feel sick?"

Mom wiggled a little on the couch.

"The medicine gets rid of bad cancer cells, but sometimes it picks on the good cells and makes them weak. This might sound a little funny, but Mrs. B's hair, her eyelashes and eyebrows will probably fall out too, because of the medicine. All these things are called side effects."

I tried to think what Mrs. B would look like without hair.

"Remember when you felt sleepy when you were taking that medicine for your allergies?" Mom said. "That was a side effect. But don't worry, the side effects will go away later. Just like they did with you."

Mom explained how Mrs. B's chemotherapy would start soon and how important it was that we prayed for her. I nodded and went to sit next to Mom on the couch. Mom always smelled good —like peaches or something. She put her arm around me and squeezed a little. I don't like it when she does that in front of Jamie, but it felt good right now.

"Can I call Jamie?"

"Sure," Mom said. "Tell him he can stay over, and if you guys behave, then I'll order a pizza and wings for supper."

"Sure!"

I headed up to my room and grabbed my iphone to text Jamie.

Hey. Are you coming over? Bring your stuff. We can play PS.

Cool...I'll be there soon, Jamie wrote.

Pizza, if you hurry! LOL.

I wished Jamie would move his tail and get here. My brain was doing dumb things. I tried not to, but I kept thinking about cancer and Mrs. B. How come cancer has to hurt people? I was afraid that Mrs. B was gonna' die. If Mrs. B dies, then I won't know how to spell very well. I could fail my math like I was doing before I started going to her. And I would miss her very much, because she is really nice to me.

Chapter 5 CHANGES

Almost five weeks passed. I had not seen Mrs. B since the hospital visit. She had sent e-mails to Mom letting us know how she was doing, and once she sent me a funny e-card with dancing medicine bottles. I missed her and I wondered sometimes what was happening. I still wanted to do something to help but didn't have a clue what I could do.

Then one day she called. Mom talked on the telephone for a while.

"Mrs. B is going to try teaching again," Mom told me when she got off the phone. I was really glad to hear that, although that meant I would have homework, and that didn't make me happy. But, I guess I would do it for Mrs. B.

"Is the cancer gone? Is she better now?" I asked Mom.

Mom looked at me. "Not yet. Mrs. B is still getting her chemotherapy. She has to have treatments for five more months."

"But how can she teach me if she still has cancer?" I asked.

"Mrs. B is going to teach her students on the days she is feeling good. She misses everyone."

Thinking about seeing Mrs. B again made me happy. I had worked on my fish story and had given cool names to all the fish. I hope Mrs. B picks some of my names for the fish. I think she will like my story.

"There are some things you need to know about Mrs. B, Tristan, before you see her again."

Uh-oh. That didn't sound good. Mom told me to sit down because we needed to have a chat. I sat on the couch.

"Mrs. B wants you to know that all her hair fell out because of the side effects of the medicine. Remember we talked about it a while ago? Now it's happened, but she doesn't want you to be scared."

It was sort of funny thinking of Mrs. B's hair falling out. But I didn't want to laugh. I would be in big trouble with Mom.

"Mrs. B also has to be careful when she is around people now because she can pick up germs easily. So when you go to her house you have to make sure you wash your hands and use a special sanitizer afterwards."

"What will happen if I don't?" I looked at my dirty hands and thought about how I sometimes forget to wash them.

"Mrs. B might get sick."

"She is sick already. Will her cancer get worse if I don't wash my hands?"

Mom stroked my head. "No, her cancer won't get worse, but if she gets a cold or gets sick to her stomach because she picks up a germ, then her treatments might be delayed."

I didn't want that to happen. All I want is for Mrs. B to get better so everything will be the same as it was before.

"Yes, I'll make sure I wash my hands and put that sanny stuff on too."

I got my hair buzzed last summer and I loved it. I liked the way it felt when I rubbed my hand over my head. I really liked it when my hair started growing back. The bristles were prickly and sharp. I wonder if Mrs. B would let me touch her head. I hope she will ask me to, because I don't wanna' ask her.

I'd been finding math hard in school lately, but I didn't tell Mom. She would have talked to Mr. Sparks and then I'd have even more homework. So I was glad in a way that I would be doing lessons with Mrs. B again. She shows me different ways to do my work and she explains things slowly. I also needed to do better in my spelling. I failed the last two dictations. Mom wasn't happy about that. I even tried standing on my head to spell when I was studying for the test, but I kept forgetting the words. It'll be better when Mrs. B is back.

"When am I going to her house?" I asked Mom.

"She wants to start teaching next Monday, so plan on going after school again like you did before.

In a way I was excited. I had read some books over the past weeks, so Mrs. B would probably let me put stickers on the squares on my reading incentive card. Maybe I will have a full line and then I can look in the treasure box and pick out a treat.

"Go check your Mrs. B bag, Tristan, and make sure you have everything caught up and ready for when you go back next week. Did you finish naming your fish? How about the story?

I grabbed my bag from the closet and pulled out the binder. I'd named all the fish. I thought my names were really cool —Raphael, Nemo, Frank, Bella, Apple Pie and Scooby. My story needed an ending though. I was having trouble figuring out how to finish it. Maybe Mrs. B would help. I decided to wait and talk to her about it.

"Okay Mom," I said. "I found my bag; everything was in it.. I even remembered to put in the last math sheet. I hope I got it right."

I clipped the buckle on my bag and thought about what it would be like to get back to my tutoring sessions. If Mrs. B was back to teaching me, did that mean she wasn't going to die from cancer? I thought everyone died who had cancer. Sometimes I get so confused.

Chapter 6 HAIRLESS

On Monday school dragged on. At three-thirty, Mom picked me up and took me to Mrs. B's for my tutoring session. I was looking forward to seeing her again, and seeing what she looked like without hair. I hoped I didn't laugh when I saw her.

"Are you gonna' come in with me, Mom?" I asked.

"Sure, if you want me to."

I wasn't scared of Mrs. B. I just didn't know what I would say. Especially if she didn't have any hair. Maybe she'd be sad. It's okay for boys to be bald. But it's weird for ladies.

Instead of dropping me off at Mrs. B's like she usually does, Mom came in with me and said she would stay for my session. It was only going to be an hour today, so she said she would read a book while she waited. Sometimes I don't like it when Mom comes, because she gives me funny looks if I don't sit still.

But today was okay. Mrs. B had a student just before me and she was saying goodbye to her. Shawna. I know her from church. Her family has a lot of kids and they homeschool. Shawna told me she gets help from Mrs. B for a few hours each day. Shawna is not a very good reader. She hardly reads in Sunday School class.

I couldn't help but stare at Mrs. B as she was talking to Shawna. She winked at me when I came in. I hate to say it, but Mrs. B looked different. She had a red scarf on her head, but I could tell she had no hair.

I took off my backpack and went to the desk where I usually sit. Mom settled herself on the couch in the classroom. I twisted around on the chair and looked at the fish. Then I remembered my story and the chart. I dug them out of my backpack and even found the math worksheet. It looked a little crumpled, but at least it was finished.

Shawna scooted out the door and Mrs. B turned to look at me. She had on her usual big smile, but she sure didn't look the same. I kind of wanted to laugh, but at the same time I felt bad for her. Also Mom would have been really mad at me if I did laugh at Mrs. B. Mom got up and gave her a hug.

"Hi Tristan!" Mrs. B said.

"Hi." I was still looking at her.

"Do you want to see my bald head?"

I sort of did and sort of didn't.

"Um…maybe."

Mrs. B. took off her scarf.

"Do I look funny without hair?"

"Yes," I said. "How does it feel?"

"Do you want to touch it?" Mrs. B asked.

I knew what my hair felt like when I had a really short haircut. But her head was shiny and looked smooth. I didn't see any bristles. When Mrs. B stuck her head close, I felt it. It wasn't at all prickly. It felt smooth. I rubbed it a little and then Mrs. B. laughed. Mom laughed too.

"It does feel a little odd, doesn't it?" said Mrs. B. "My eyelashes and eyebrows are starting to fall out too, so soon I will be as bald as a plucked chicken.

Mom laughed and went to sit down again.

"Cool." I couldn't think of anything else to say.

Mrs. B liked my ideas for fish names and she told me she had started a chart for the different suggestions. She would look at them and decide what she liked once all of her students had shared their ideas. The deadline for suggestions was tomorrow. I was glad I had mine in on time.

Mrs. B thought my fish tale was a good one. We worked on some good ideas for endings. Part of my homework assignment—finish my fish story.

Mrs. B didn't laugh as much or tell jokes like before. Sometimes, during our time together, she rubbed her feet and legs. At one point—I don't think Mom saw her, but I did—she made a face like she was in pain, and then she rubbed the side of her leg. I'm kind of thinking she wasn't too well, because she forgot to ask me about my math worksheet. I didn't mind if she forgot about it though. Soon it was time to go home. My next session would be in two days.

"Are you okay?" Mom asked Mrs. B as we were leaving.

"I guess I'm just a little tired. But I have four more students this evening, so I had better get over it!" Mrs. B said and then smiled her usual big grin.

We left. Mom didn't say much on the way home. I thought about a good ending for my fish story.

Chapter 7 CANCELLED?

The shrill ring made me jump out of my skin.

"I'll get it!" I yelled from the kitchen.

"Hello," I said.

"Tristan. Good to hear your voice. How are you today?"

I recognized Mrs. B's voice on the phone right away.

"Good."

"Is your Mom there, please?"

"Yes. Hold on a sec'" I covered the receiver with my hand.

"Mom! Mrs. B wants to speak to you!"

"Got it," she called back from somewhere upstairs.

I listened for a minute until Mom told me to hang up the phone. I wondered if my tutoring session was cancelled. I kind of hoped so. I still needed to finish reading a couple of chapters in my last book. I went back to my computer.

A while later Mom came downstairs and went into the kitchen. I closed the window on my game and followed her.

"What did Mrs. B want?" I was still hoping she had cancelled my Thursday session.

"Oh, hi," she said looking surprised I was there. "Well there's more news about Mrs. B."

"Uh-oh," I said. I started to feel a little guilty for wishing my session was being cancelled. The smell from the turnips bubbling on the stove didn't help my churning stomach much.

"Mrs. B is not going to be teaching..."

"Is she dying?" I blurted it out before I could even think.

Mom tipped the lid on the turnips. Then she turned around and looked at me.

"Let me finish, Tristan. No, Mrs. B is not dying. She isn't going to be teaching for a while though. She's finding that teaching is too tiring right now. So we're going to wait until she has finished all her treatments. That way she can rest when she feels like it."

I was glad to hear that Mrs. B was not dying. I was also a little relieved about having lots of time to finish my reading.

"But," Mom interrupted my guilty thoughts, "you are still going to be getting some work from Mrs. B."

"I am?"

"Mrs. B said she is willing to continue with your lessons via the Internet."

"Huh? What do you mean?" I had a feeling I wasn't going to be getting out of finishing those two chapters in my book after all.

"Mrs. B said she will make an audio file of what you have to do and she will prepare some worksheets. She'll send the files and any worksheets to us each Monday and then we will download everything. You will work on the lessons using the audio file as your guide. We'll send the completed lessons back to her the following week and then she will send new assignments."

"Really? So I still have to do extra work?" I said, using my not-so-thrilled voice.

"We'll give it a try for now. Mrs. B also said you can use

e-mail to send lessons or ask questions."

I didn't have much of a choice. So I told myself to have a good attitude and to just do it.

"How long for?" I asked.

"Just a few months."

For some dumb reason I thought about Mrs. B's fish. She still hadn't said anything about the names. Maybe she hadn't decided yet. Maybe she hadn't felt like naming the fish. But I still wondered all the same.

"Can you e-mail Mrs. B for me, Mom?"

"Right now?"

"Sure."

"How come?"

"I want to know if she picked out any of the names I suggested for the fish."

Mom grinned. "You e-mail her. This can be practice for when you send your lessons."

Maybe Mom had a good idea. I needed to start e-mailing her anyway. I had Mrs. B's address on my computer from when she sent me a card. I pressed Create Mail and then typed in Mrs. B. Her address popped up.

Hi, Mrs. Beeeeeee (She would laugh at that) *I hope you are fine. I am fine. Mom says you are going to send me stuff to do at home. What are you calling the fish? I hope you pick the names I made up. Thanks. Bye. From Tristan.*

Mom called me to come to the kitchen because dinner was ready. Yippee…turnip. My favorite – Not!

Chapter 8 SOMETHING FISHY

Hello Tristan,

Thanks for sending me a message on e-mail. I like it when I get messages. I am feeling good today. I have your lesson ready for this week. Mom said she's downloading things without a problem. Yay! I hope these audio files are okay for you. Don't laugh at my squeaky voice. Do your best on the homework. That's all I ask.

About the fish, I have some good news and some bad news and then some more good news. The first good news is that I named all the fish in the aquarium. The bad news is I came down to the classroom this morning and there were eight fish floating upside down in the water. I felt so bad. I had cleaned them out yesterday but I must have done something wrong. Do you want to know the last good news? I had picked two of your names – "Apple Pie" for the tiniest one and "Raphael" for the biggest one. And guess what? They are the ones that did not die. How about that? Next time you come you can say hello to them and see what a fine team they are. I am going to be more careful. I think I will call the pet shop to find out how to properly look after them. I really had no idea. Maybe I should just stick to teaching! Take care. I hope to see you soon.

Mrs. B.

It was nice to get a message from Mrs. B, but I was sad about the eight fish that died. I was glad that Apple Pie and Raphael were still alive though. That was neat that the ones I named didn't get flushed down the toilet, like she did with the other fish.

****

School drove me crazy today. My locker stuck. I forgot my book at home and got into big trouble, and I accidentally ripped a page in my agenda and got into trouble again. "Accidents happen," I said a little too loud around Mr. Sparks. Sitting on the blue bench outside the office was not a good way to end my day.

Mom told me Mrs. B sent some more lessons along with my corrected ones from last time.

In one way I looked forward to getting the audio files and stuff. But I really wasn't crazy about the homework even though I wanted to listen to what Mrs. B said.

I did my homework both from school and from Mrs. B. I somehow get more Mrs. B homework. What's with that? She likes to keep drilling until I get it. Whatever.

I saw something cool today on TV. It was some kind of fundraiser. A bunch of people were running to help raise money for cancer. The commercial was only a few minutes, but it made me happy in one way and sad in another. They talked about people dying from cancer. Watching that commercial made me think about Mrs. B. It would be so cool to do something for her. Maybe I could run or do something to help raise some money to help her get better.

"No TV while you're doing homework!" Mom yelled from the office.

"I'm done," I said.

She doesn't get it. Just because she has to have silence when she works doesn't mean I have to.

I pulled my phone out of my pocket and texted Jamie.

Hey U! What's up? Question...what r u doing 2nite?

Jamie didn't answer right away so I played this mind maze thing. It's supposed to be good for my brain.

Hey!

He texted me back after a few minutes. I was already at level 9. My goal was 11.

Sup?

Thinking...LOL

Uh-oh...what does that mean?

It's about Mrs. B.

She's cool. Sorry she's got cancer. That sucks.

Ya. It sure does. Wanna' help me with something?

What?

I have this brainiac idea, but I'm not sure how to actually do it. Jamie goes to the same church as me and he knows Mrs. B, because she taught him Sunday School once. So I thought he might like to help.

Can you come over later and I'll tell you?

I'll ask.

I didn't hear any more so I figured Jamie was asking his mom if he could come over. As I was waiting for him to message me back I got another text from Miranda.

Hey! How R U?

Miranda Noble is another of Mrs. B's students. She and her twin sister Michaela go on Tuesdays and Thursdays I think.

Good.

I was surprised to get a text from her. She doesn't talk to me a lot, but she did ask for my number when I got my iphone for my 12th birthday last month.

What's up? she asked.

Bad day at school.

LOL

I told her, although she probably already knew since she had seen me sitting outside the office earlier. She answered back right away.

I figured as much when I saw U sitting on the blue bench.

Never mind. It was dumb. Mr. S was just being mean.

S'okay. I heard.

I didn't want to talk about it anymore so I changed the subject.

Did you know about Mrs. B?

Yes. That's horrible. I can't go to her place for tutoring right now, but she's sending me HW

R U using the computer? Audio files and stuff?

Nope.

How come?

Dunno...my mom just picks up the list and the stuff I'm supposed to do. Sometimes she sends worksheets on my email. So guess what? Michaela and I are doing something to help with her cancer.

I sat up when she said that.

What are you guys doing?

It's our birthday next Friday. We're inviting a bunch of people. But we're gonna' tell them to bring money for our Mrs. B Jar of Hope, instead of bringing us a present.

I thought that was a pretty cool thing to do and it kinda' worked out with what I wanted to talk to Jamie about.

Cool. I'm doing something too.

My brain was going a mile a minute. Then Jamie texted.

K. I can come over for a while. You done your hw? Mom freaked out at first and said I had to check that you didn't have homework. So I am checking bro. Done?

Yuppers. I wrote and laughed at Jamie calling me bro! He's like a bro 'cept he has a better tan than me!

My phone dinged again. It was Miranda.

So what are you doing for Mrs. B?

I didn't feel like writing everything down so I asked Miranda if she wanted to come over for a while too.

I hoped Jamie wouldn't mind.

Buddy...you don't mind if I ask Miranda to come to my place too, do ya? I wanna' tell you guys my idea 'cause I need some major help. LOL.

Sure thing. What about asking Mickey Mouse too?

Mickey-Michaela? Sure. No prob. Hold on. I'll ask.

Right before I did that I yelled at Mom. I didn't want her to freak out about all these people beating down our door! Mom is pretty cool most of the time. She said it was okay.

I wrote back: *Bring Mickey too, if you want. The more, the better.*

Miranda messaged me back and said they would be able to come in about half an hour.

Perfect. See you then.

I told Jamie to get his butt over here as soon as possible. We had work to do. Good work. But work all the same.

All Jamie wrote was *LOL!*

Chapter 9 THE CANCEL CANCER PARTY

"Hey!" Jamie yelled at me when he came around the corner. I was in the garage pulling my bike off the wall.

"Hey!" I said.

We chatted a while about my new- to- me bike I got (or I should say Mom got) at an auction sale. When Miranda and Mickey came, I showed them the very cool secret compartment on the back of my bike. It looked like a water bottle, but when you pressed the button, the top popped up and you could keep stuff in there.

"Way cool," said Miranda. Mickey just grinned. She wasn't real talkative.

"I want one of those!" Jamie said. "Sheesh...and from an auction. Who'd of guessed?"

The four of us hung out for a while. I told them Mom said we could grab a drink from the outside fridge. We did and then went into the backyard to talk about my plan.

"So? What's your idea?" Jamie asked.

"Okay," I said. "I was thinking that we should have a Cancel Cancer party for Mrs. B. And then the money we earn could go to the Cancer Society and maybe we could get her a present too. We could get all her students and their families and maybe a few other people to come and we could have games and stuff. Then we could have a competition to see who gets their head shaved.

"Maybe we could make a game and get someone to shave his or her head," Miranda said. I ran my fingers through my curly hair and thought how being totally bald would feel really weird.

"Great idea!" Mickey said. Jamie liked the idea, too. "So, do you want to come to our birthday party next week? We can tell everyone there about the Cancel Cancer party."

"Sure. You guys should come!" Miranda said.

I was pretty happy the twins invited Jamie and me to their birthday party. And I was happy that Mickey was getting excited about the plans too.

"Any other boys going?" I asked

"Sam, Juan, Ethan…" Mickey said.

"K. I'll ask Mom."

"I'll ask and text you later," said Jamie.

I was pretty impressed with the twins saying that having a competition to shave heads would be a good idea. What if one of them lost, or I guess, won? They're girls and they've both got long hair. I'll freak out if I have to get it done and I'm a guy. It would be even easier for Jamie, since his hair is not that long. Although I remember last year he said he would never get a buzz cut. I would laugh so much if he had to get his head shaved.

Two hours later we had a lot figured out. Miranda wrote notes about what we have to do. Both girls said they would arrange the food for the party and Jamie and I could look after the games. We decided on a dart game, a catch-the-rubber-duck-in-the-pool game and a bunch of guessing games. The problem was figuring out prizes. Each of us decided we would ask our parents for ideas.

"We have to leave," Micky said, poking her sister in the arm. "We said we wouldn't be that long."

"Yup. Me, too," said Jamie, reaching for his vibrating phone. "My mom just texted me and said I had to come home. I'd better go and I'll let you know about the party."

"Thanks for coming!" I yelled as the three left on their bikes. I took one last spin on my bike around the block, then went in the house.

"MOM!"

"Do you have to scream?" Mom said, pretending to be startled.

"So how did your planning go?"

I told her what we wanted to do and about Jamie and me getting invited to Miranda and Mickey's party. I also told her about the head shaving competition. She said I could go to the party and she also came up with an idea.

"Why don't you make the head shaving competition sort of like a silent auction?"

"Huh? What's a silent auction?" My brain was telling me that there was nothing silent about the auction where we got my bike. In fact it was the opposite. I remembered everyone yelling and calling out bids on things.

Mom grinned and explained that a silent auction is when items are written on a piece of paper and then people write down their bids. "It would be a little different, but what if you wrote down the name of each person willing to get their head shaved, and then people could bid."

Mom's idea was starting to sound good.

"We could charge $1 a bid," I said.

"Good idea!" Mom said. "Stick a signup sheet and a jar beside each page."

I was liking this idea a lot. "Then when we call a cut-off time, then the person with the most names on the page is the loser...um...winner?"

"Guess that depends on how you look at it." Mom smiled and told me to get cleaned up for supper.

I quickly texted Miranda and Jamie. They both answered the same at first.

LOL

LOL

Then Miranda texted me again: *I LOVE that idea. Now all we have to do is find out who wants to put their names on the sign-up sheet. Who's gonna do the shaving, by the way?*

Shoot, I never thought of that. Then I remembered that Shawna's mom was a hairdresser. Maybe I could ask Shawna to ask her Mom. But Shawna doesn't text so I would have to call her. I decided to see if Miranda would talk to her.

Miranda replied right away. *No problem! She's coming to our party on Friday anyway. So we can ask her then.*

That was a relief. I would feel dumb asking Shawna if her Mom knew how to shave heads.

Good idea and I can come to your party, I texted back. I was heading into the bathroom when the phone rang.

"Trist. It's for you. Jamie!"

"Got it." I grabbed the phone in the hall.

"Miss me already?" I grinned and caught a glimpse of my crazy hair in the mirror. I secretly hoped I wouldn't win the head-shaving competition. I liked my mop.

"Um...we never talked about where we were going to do this, Doofus."

I laughed and decided that we really should figure that out first. Mom heard us talking and motioned for me to hang up the phone.

"Gotta run. I'll call you later," I said.

"Okay. Hey, I can go to the party!"

"Good. Me, too! See you later." I pressed the off button.

"I told you five minutes ago that supper was ready," Mom said.

"I know," I mumbled, tucking my phone in my pocket. Mom freaks out if I have it on the table.

"Do you want to say grace?" Mom smiled at me as if she had something to say.

"Okay." I wondered what else she was cooking up besides supper.

"Thank you, God, for this day, this time and for what we have. Help Mrs. B get through her chemo treatments and help her to get better. Thank you for friends, family and food. Amen!"

"Amen…" Mom echoed. "So I heard you talking to Jamie about the party."

I nodded and put a forkful of potatoes in my mouth.

"You can have it here, if you want. I can clear out the garage and we can set everything up inside and if the weather is okay, outside too."

I really thought Mom wouldn't want all kinds of people running around. She likes her quiet. So I was happy that she said it was okay.

“Hey Mom. Are you going to sign up to get your hair buzzed too?” I shoved another forkful of potatoes in my mouth. Mom grinned.

“Maybe.”

Chapter 10 THE BIRTHDAY PLAN

Finally it was Friday. I especially wanted Friday to hurry up and come this week because it's Miranda's and Mickey's birthday party and we could figure stuff out and ask Shawna about her mom helping out with the head-shaving contest. I had told Jamie that we could pick him up. Mom said she would give us both a ride to the girls' house and then Jamie could stay overnight here after the party. Jamie's parents agreed.

That was cool. Then we could do some more planning and also get caught up on our gaming tournament. I really needed to conquer level 12 before Jamie!

Jamie and I got out of the car. Mom told me to text her when the party was over and she would come and pick us up. It was supposed to be over around 10, but I told Mom we might be a little late if we got talking about the Cancel Cancer party for Mrs. B.

When we walked in the door, it was a little freaky. It seemed like there were 100 girls. There were actually only 10, but it seemed like more. Ethan was in a corner talking to Juan. There was no sign of Sam.

"Hey!" Miranda and Mickey came to the door and seemed happy to see us. Just as we deposited our 'gift money' in the Mrs. B jar, the doorbell rang. It was Sam. He was grinning and holding a huge cake. Jamie and I laughed.

Sam wants to be a chef. All he talks about is cooking shows on TV and he often tells us about the different meals he would make for his family. He could never be satisfied with a plain old hamburger. He had to fancy it up with weird cheese, sautéed mushrooms and other strange stuff.

Some of us think he is a little odd because he isn't into video games and sports very much. But hey, Sam is Sam. Sam is actually really smart and funny. If people tease him, he always has a snappy comeback – Sam I am Sam; I am Sam; I really like that Sam I am! You don't like me? I don't care 'cause I am Sam so you can scram! Can you tell he is a Dr. Seuss fan?

The girls were all over Sam, telling him what a cool cake he had made for the party. I started to think that maybe I should take up cooking. The cake actually was pretty cool. It had two round cakes on top of each other with some fancy white icing. On the top lay this huge flower made out of green, yellow and white icing. It looked like a daisy and then there were a whole bunch of little yellow and white daisies sticking out of the sides of the cake. The green icing around the bottom of each layer looked like grass and the daisies were yellow and white. I'm not big on flowers, but Sam did a good job and Miranda and Mickey were sure impressed.

Everyone enjoyed the party and the food disappeared quickly, including the daisy cake. We played a game outside. I don't know the name, but we had these weights on strings that you had to throw and try to get them to wrap around this bar. The competition got pretty good, and it sure pulled us boys out of the corner. Juan ended up winning, but quiet Shawna was a pretty close second. We had to quit when it got dark.

It was getting close to 10 when Miranda told everyone about our Cancel Cancer party idea. She thanked everyone for bringing money for the Mrs. B jar. Mickey counted it and there was $145.00. We all cheered. Quite a few kids seemed really interested in helping out, so we told them our plan. Miranda asked Shawna if she thought her mother would shave the head of the silent auction winner. Shawna said she probably would, but she would ask. We all decided that before we would give the profits from the fundraiser to the Cancer Society, we would get a gift for Mrs. B. It would be really nice to get her something personal—something to remind her of the day. All we had to do was figure out what to get.

We talked about all kinds of things. Sam stuck around too. He offered to make some cake pops and some awareness ribbon cookies to sell. Miranda told him to make everything a teal colour, because that was the colour for ovarian cancer. By the time Mom picked up Jamie and me at 10:45, our brains were in overdrive.

On the way home Jamie and I told Mom the plans. "This thing is turning into quite a party," Mom said. "Good job we have a big back yard."

She was right. The games would take up quite a bit of room. We decided to put the dart board on the shed; Jamie said we could borrow his kid sister's wading pool for the fishing for ducks game, but we didn't want to put that too close to the dart board — stray darts would definitely ruin the fun. Mom told me earlier that she would put some money towards buying things for the guessing game and she could also help out with prizes too.

When we got home, Mom handed Jamie and me an envelope. We opened it quickly.

"Wow! Mom…are you serious? $100?"

Jamie grinned. I hugged her.

"Thanks so much. This will really help."

We told her our plans to buy gummy worms, balloons and fish crackers for the guessing games. Shawna, Miranda, Mickey and I thought fish crackers would be funny. Mrs. B would laugh. Jamie didn't get it at first until we explained Mrs. B's fish tank fiasco to him. Mom also said she would take photos that day and even offered to set up a little photo booth where people could pay $5 and get their picture taken. Mom said she would give everyone a 5 x 7 print for that and then the rest of the money would be donated to the day. We could hardly wait to tell the girls. I texted Miranda.

We decided to have the party a week from tomorrow. That way we would have time to invite some kids. We would put up posters and tell everyone to tell their friends. Some said they would tell their parents and then they could spread the word.

Miranda answered back. It's gonna' be sunny…and that is so awesome about the photo booth.

Jamie and I did a high five and talked for a while about who would do what. Then we got out our game controls, put our baseball caps on backward and got serious about who would get to the next level first.

Chapter 11 DOLLARS AND SENSE

After breakfast we talked to Mom about going to get the stuff for the guessing games, and we could also see what we could buy for prizes. We were in the process of figuring out where we could go and the phone rang.

"I'll get it!" Mom said.

Jamie and I decided we would head out on our bikes to the bulk food store to get the candy. I knew Mom had jars we could use for the guessing games. We would drop off at the discount store after to pick up some prizes.

"Hey, Buddy!" Mom yelled from the kitchen. "Go check your computer!"

When Mom calls me 'Buddy' that means there is either good news or I'm in trouble. By the sound of her voice, I think I was okay this time. I went to the computer.

"Where do you want me to look?"

"Check my Facebook page. It's open!" Mom said.

I clicked the mouse.. I couldn't believe my eyes. Miranda's mother had started an event on her Facebook page and had invited all sorts of people to come. So far she had 23 friends saying they would definitely be attending. There were 12 people who said they could not attend but three of those had made comments.

So sorry we can't make it but I would like to donate $50...

Sorry, we are out of town but can I give some money to help? How about $25?...

I would love to come but we have a family reunion next Saturday. We usually pick something every year to donate to *so this year we pick you! How does $200 sound? If you can get us a receipt that would be nice. If not, don't worry about it. Let me know when you need the money...*

Jamie and I jumped around like a couple of excited kindergarteners.

"That's $275! Do you believe it?" Jamie said in a high voice.

"And with Mom's $100, then we have $375 before we even start!"

Mom came into the living room beaming like an Olympic medalist on the podium.

"That was Miranda's mom. We are pretty proud of you guys, you know." Mom put her fist forward and we all gave each other 'props.'

"Should we tell Mrs. B?" I asked Mom and wanted to know what Jamie thought too.

Both Jamie and Mom said we definitely should since she is the star attraction. We had planned the date, but we forgot to ask Mrs. B if it suited her! Mom told me I should call her right away. I was sort of chicken to call and asked Mom if it was okay if she would. She gave me that look again and told me that since I was the chief organizer, I should make the call.

Just as I was about to pick up the phone, Miranda texted me.

Did you see what Mrs. B said?

I quick texted back and asked Miranda what she was talking about.

Check FB

When I looked on Mom's Facebook homepage, I saw it.

"What are those kids up to?" Mrs. B had typed in a row of smiley faces. I guess she had seen the post.

I told Miranda that I was going to call Mrs. B and tell her all about our plans.

At first I felt a little awkward talking to Mrs. B about the Cancel Cancer party. But she was so excited that I quickly forgot about how nervous I was. I ended up putting her on speaker phone and both Jamie and I told her about the day. We didn't want to tell her everything. She went quiet when we told her that all the money we raise will go to the Cancer Society.

"I don't know what to say," she said.

I kind of chuckled inside at that, because Mrs. B usually knows what to say.

We talked for a while and Jamie and I were glad to find out that, although Mrs. B wasn't feeling the greatest because of some of the side effects of her chemo, she said that wild horses wouldn't keep her away. Kind of a weird thing to say, I thought, but I think it meant that she was definitely coming to the Cancel Cancer party on Saturday.

Saturday was going to be a crazy day. Mom talked to Mickey and Miranda's parents, and a little later on, Shawna's mom called to say that she would be happy to shave the head of the person who gets the most votes. Mrs. Noble told Mom she would also like to donate $100 to help with expenses. Things just kept getting better and better. Jamie's parents offered to buy three cases of water and some juice for refreshments. Mrs. Jackson said she would bake some muffins and also her famous white chocolate cheesecake.

We had so much to do, but all the same, we could hardly wait for Saturday to come. I tried to do my homework for school and for Mrs. B, but it was hard. Even harder was paying attention in class. It was so tempting to pull out my phone and text everyone when I had a thought or another idea. But I couldn't take a chance of losing my phone or getting a blast from Sir Sparks and spending more time on the dreaded blue bench.

Friday was here and there was still stuff to do. But Miranda and Mickey had all the sign-up sheets ready for the head-shaving silent auction. I had the pens, the donation jars, and Mom had made labels of those who dared to get their head shaved. Jamie was staying overnight, so he helped me put the stickers on the jars. Tristan Hauser, Jamie Jackson, Miranda Noble, Michaela Noble, Sam Bellaire, Shawna Newton and…we stopped in our tracks when we saw the last two names – Renee Jackson and Pat Hauser. We laughed our heads off as we imagined our mothers bald.

"Buddy!"

The clock chimed 7pm. Mom had answered the phone about five minutes ago, so I figured something was up. Her tone of voice this time sounded a little uptight.

"Tristan, that was Mrs. B on the phone. She had something come up, so she is just giving you the heads up that she might be late tomorrow."

I understood because sometimes Mrs. B gets tired really quickly. Maybe she didn't want to say that. But I would still feel awful if she couldn't make it to the party for some reason. I thought about the wild horses.

When I told Jamie about Mrs. B, he didn't say much at first.

"Um, well…" Jamie eventually said, "We will still have fun and we'll try our best to raise lots of money, even if Mrs. B can't make it. Everyone will understand."

Chapter 12 GRAHAM

The party was scheduled to begin at 1 and run for the whole afternoon. Miranda, Mickey, Shawna and Sam came over around nine o'clock Saturday morning to help us set up. My prayers about the weather had been answered. The sun had already warmed up our big back yard, and we were glad we had borrowed a few shade umbrellas for the afternoon. Mom had arranged for a babysitter to look after Gillian, so she was available to help out wherever we needed her. She had already set up her little photo booth under a pop-up tent, and even though I am not big on glitzy stuff, I will say it looked pretty cool with all the teal hats and feathers and a couple of neat stools and stuff. Mom had made a background from brown fabric that sort of looked like barn boards. Sam volunteered to put up his homemade signs in the front yard and down the street so everyone would know this was the place.

We had all decided that we would have a prize table, so whenever anyone won something, they could exchange a ticket for a prize. Shawna had made up a bunch of tickets, so she handed some to Jamie and me, because we were looking after the games. For the guessing games, we didn't need tickets. People would look at the jar and try to guess the number of balloons, gummy worms and fish crackers and then write their answer on the sheet next to each jar for 25 cents a guess. I was sad Mrs. B might not be able to see the fish crackers. She would have laughed at those.

Jamie said he would look after the darts. People could pay 50 cents to play — score ten or more with three darts and you win a prize. I would look after the rubber duck game and we could both help out with the guessing game. It was fun filling up the pond with the hose. I was so tempted to spray Jamie. We put in fifteen rubber ducks that we had bought at the discount store— three for a dollar. We had numbered them one to 15 with a marker. All even numbers would win a prize. They looked pretty cute bobbing up and down in the plastic pond.

Miranda and Mickey had set up all the tables. They had bought some teal plastic tablecloths so everything matched. The prize table was next to the photo booth and the girls had everything ready. Sam was pretty proud of his cake pops with teal sprinkles and the awareness ribbon-shaped cookies. Only Sam could do that. He would probably sell out in no time once we started.

The girls had also made a very cool banner that said CANCEL CANCER; WE LOVE YOU MRS. B. It hung on the fence where people came in. I sure hoped Mrs. B could make it. I wanted her to see all this.

"Mom!" I suddenly remembered something. "Did you remember to pick up Mrs. B's present?

"Don't worry. Got it."

I wracked my brain trying to think if we had forgotten anything. Shawna would watch the snack table and keep it filled as people helped themselves. She would also keep her eye on the silent auction. A long table situated next to the special 'haircutting' chair, held jars with ribbons, sheets of paper and pens. The open jars beckoned people to toss in a dollar next to the name of their favorite 'victim'. Mom had bought some helium-filled balloons and had tied two to the back of the chair. I touched my curly mop again and told myself that if I get picked to shave my head, then it would be for a great cause!

It wasn't even one o'clock and people started arriving. Before we knew it our backyard was bustling with people. I knew most of them although there were some faces I didn't recognize. I think all of Mrs. B's students and their families were here. One family who homeschooled had ten children. They practically filled up the yard themselves.

Everyone seemed to have fun with the games. When I wasn't too busy with the duck pond, I scooted over to the silent auction table to see what was happening. There were five signatures on Jamie's page and seven on mine. The twins had a few and Sam and Shawna each had four. But the best part was, Mom had nine and Mrs. Jackson had ten! I told Jamie. We howled.

Tons of people had played the guessing games, and we even had to go get another sheet for the fish crackers. The quarters were piling up. I was just helping David, one of Mrs. B's students, to fish out a duck with the net, when I heard someone yell my name.

"Hey, Tristan!"

I looked around. The voice sounded familiar. I looked toward the fence and to my surprise, I saw Mrs. B. I was so happy to see her, although it wasn't Mrs. B's voice I was hearing. I went to see Mrs. B. She gave me a big hug, and everyone stopped playing the games and visiting with each other. But it was the other face that got my heart beating louder than a train on a mission. I couldn't believe my eyes.

Mom and Mrs. B had their arms around each other as they watched me.

"Graham? Graham Deeble?"

"Hey, Trist. How's things?"

I wanted to faint. I wanted to cry. I wanted to give my old friend a great big hug.

"What are you doing here?" was all I could muster for words.

Chapter 13 BUZZ JOBS

Then the chatter started. Everyone but me knew that Mrs. B had arranged for Graham to come to the party. I found out later that Mrs. B was so grateful to me for organizing everything she wanted to find a special way to say thank you. And special this was. When Graham's mom died of cancer two years ago and they ended up moving 200 kms away, I was so sad. I never thought I would see Graham again. Jamie, 'Gray' and I had been a fearless threesome growing up together. The teacher called us the Terrifically Terrifying Trio in Grade One when we pretended we were superheroes. We didn't know what that meant at the time, but we knew we were a team.

Now Mrs. B was the superhero. I was so happy to see my old friend, and better yet, I found out that Graham's dad might get his old job back, which meant they might move back to town.

"Thanks, Mrs. B," I said. "Are you feeling okay? I thought you were sick and you couldn't come today."

"Are you kidding me?" she said. "Remember those wild horses?" She waved her arm in the air like a lasso. She winked at me then headed out to talk and mingle.

Mrs. B made the rounds. Sometimes she had to sit down to rest, but she did so well walking around and checking out all the fun.

Gray, Jamie and I hung out and talked like it was just last week. If Gray did move back, then it would be so cool. He said he would let us know as soon as he found out. His dad would be by to pick him up later. Gray didn't have a phone yet, but he said his Dad was talking about getting him one soon. I hoped so, and then we could stay connected.

Sam's cake pops and ribbon cookies sold out quickly, so he moved over to help Shawna serve the snacks. He eyed the white chocolate cheesecake sitting on a block of ice and was quick to ask Mrs. Jackson for the recipe.

Everyone paid attention when Miranda announced that there were five minutes left to the 4 o'clock deadline for the head-shaving contest. As if on cue, a whole bunch of people went over to the table laughing and pushing their way to the sign-up sheets. The dollars were dropping in the jars like stones off a cliff.

"Ten, nine, eight, seven, six, five, four, three, two, one…time's up!" Miranda shouted. Everyone dropped the pens and backed out of the way. One of the dads pretended to do a drum roll as Jamie and I collected the sheets. Everyone gathered around and laughed as Mrs. B read off the results.

Miranda Noble – 20; Mickey Noble – 20; Jamie Jackson – 20; Sam Bellaire – 20; Shawna Newton – 20; Renee Jackson – 20; Pat Hauser – 20; Tristan Hauser- 20!

We had been set up. There were exactly 20 names on the page and $20 in each jar. But rules were rules. In the case of an eight-way tie for first place, everyone gets a haircut!

Mrs. Newton was going to be busy for a while. Luckily, Mom had a hair-cutting set in the house. Mrs. Whale, a next door neighbor, volunteered to help out, and so a second chair was set up and the buzzing began.

It took almost 40 minutes before our heads were shaved. We all stood in a row to show Mrs. B. Tears rolled down her cheeks and she shook her head. Everyone clapped.

"Thank you…" she said. "You all look like me now!"

"Anyone want their picture taken?" Mom asked.

Before long there was a big queue at the photo booth. The first picture taken was Mrs. B and the eight shaved heads. Shawna's Mom offered to take the picture.

"I'm happy to take a picture of all my…um…volunteers!"

We all laughed and it felt so good to see Mrs. B smiling.

Chapter 14 FRANK & BELLA

Some people were getting ready to leave. Graham's dad had come so we knew he would be heading out soon. Mrs. B and Gray's dad looked like they were heavy in a conversation, but we thought it was time to make the announcement anyway. Miranda had tallied up all the money, so I let her be the one to tell the good news.

"Including some online donations and minus a few expenses, it looks like we made a grand total of $1,398.50!"

Everyone cheered.

"And I will add $101.50 to make it a nice round number!" Mr. Deeble shouted above the cheers!

'Woohoo! $1500.00!" I yelled.

Mrs. B looked at me and clapped quietly.

"Good adding, Tristan," she said for my ears only. I felt my cheeks turn red.

"Excuse me, everyone! Excuse me!" We had one more thing to do before everyone left. Jamie told Mrs. B that she had to close her eyes. I led all 11 of Mrs. B's students to our front porch. All twelve of us came out with our treasure and stood in a row. A few onlookers stifled giggles. I raised my finger to my lips to indicate 'no telling!' I nodded to Jamie as planned.

"Mrs. B, keep your eyes closed for another few seconds. Tristan has made up a song and we are all going to sing it to you, but you are not allowed to open your eyes until I tell you.

Mrs. B smiled and nodded with her eyes still closed.

We sang the song to the tune of 'Happy Birthday to You.'

Mrs. B, here's our wish,
Mrs. B, here's our wish.
We pray you get healthy
And we've bought you some...

"Okay Mrs. B...You can open your eyes now!" Jamie said.

"FISH!" Everyone yelled.

Laughter filled the backyard. Mrs. B cried again. Each one of her students stood holding a big plastic bag containing a fish very similar to the ones that had perished in her tank.

"Friends for Apple Pie and Raphael!" I said.

Mrs. B was overjoyed. "Now everyone can name their own fish," she said, wiping her eyes.

All the kids were rattling off the names of the fish, so Mickey got a piece of paper and pen and wrote them down for Mrs. B to remember. Every time someone said a name, Mrs. B would say how wonderful or clever or funny it was. What a nice lady! I really do hope she gets better soon.

People started to leave, but it took a while for everyone to say goodbye to Mrs. B. It was hard seeing Gray leave, but his dad did say they are likely moving back within the next few months, if all works out with his job. Jamie and I high-fived our friend and talked for a few minutes about getting our old clubhouse at Jamie's place fixed up again.

"Make sure you text me first when you get your phone," I told Gray loud enough for his dad to hear.

It didn't take long to clean up. Miranda, Mickey, Sam and Shawna stayed to help Jamie and me. Sam didn't have much to clean up on his table. Once everyone left, Mom offered to drive Mrs. B home because she looked pretty tired.

"You can leave your car here for now, if you like. That way we can help you with your fish."

Mrs. B thought that might be a good idea. Mom told her she would pick her up tomorrow to get her car. When we got to Mrs. B's place, I carried the fish into the house two at a time. I sure didn't want to drop any. With care, Mom and I opened each plastic bag and slipped the fish into their new watery home. Raphael and Apple Pie seemed to like their new friends.

"The aquarium doesn't look empty anymore," Mrs. B said after we finished.

She said that she had learned much about caring for fish from the man at the pet store, plus she had been reading up online about caring for fish in an aquarium. I think Mrs. B liked her presents.

"You look tired," Mom said.

"Yes, I am, but I don't want you to go yet." Mrs. B touched my shoulder in exactly the same way she had that day when she told me she had cancer.

"Tristan, you have no idea what good you have done for me."

My mouth felt dry and I didn't know what to say. My mind played dumb tricks again and I thought of how Mr. Sparks always tells me that I need to do better and get smarter and work harder. I like it when people say nice things to me, but I never know what to say.

"Each time I go for my treatment from now on, I will think about this day. I will remember the hard work you all put into making this day so special for me. Most of all, I will remember your heart."

Now Mom was wiping her eyes. I stood like an idiot not saying anything.

"Only God knows what will happen to me in the future," Mrs. B. said "I'm hoping that once this chemotherapy is over, I can get back to the business of being me. But I have to listen to the doctors and do as I am told."

It was beginning to sound a lot like school.

"Tristan, you have no idea how much you have lifted my spirits. That card you made for me when I was in hospital remains one of my most treasured possessions. When you told me in your note, that I am 'always in your heart,' I cried and was so thankful that you think of me that way."

Mom dug out a tissue. I started to feel a lump in my throat too. Mrs. B smiled at me, and for some dumb reason, I wanted to call her Grandma. I was glad no one could read my mind.

"I never had children of my own, but I feel like I have a whole houseful of kids. Thank you. I really mean that from the bottom of my heart."

"Um...," I fumbled for just the right words... "Um...you can call the fish I was holding... Frank and Bella."

Choose:

- ✓Life
- ✓Love
- ✓Kindness
- ✓Hope

About the Author:

Glynis has many passions but what keeps her going is inspiration from the everyday along with an attitude of gratitude.

As a happy, busy writer, children's author and publisher, Glynis's days are filled with sunshine, hope and a thousand reasons to be grateful. She is notorious for turning lemons into lemonade and dancing out loud even if everyone is looking.

She enjoys words and when they cling together to inspire, bring hope and encourage, Glynis counts her writing a success.